Recreational

Dungeness Crabbing

by Scott Haugen

Recreational
Dungeness Crabbing

by Scott Haugen

Frank
Amato
PORTLAND

Dedication

This book is dedicated to my son, Kazden. When I was a young boy, my dad would take me crabbing, instilling a desire to pursue these joyous creatures at a very young age. I vividly recall the pots being pulled to the surface, anticipation mounting as I yearned to see what we'd caught.

Not only did the uncertainty of the size and number of crabs appearing in each pot boost my enthusiasm, but the opportunity to toss back a dozen undersized creatures kept me wanting more. Reaching into a pot full of scurrying little crabs, their pincers nipping at my fingertips, was as thrilling for me as placing keepers in the cooler. Better yet were the times rings were hoisted aboard, spilling out crabs that scurried about the bottom of the craft. Frantically moving to seize and

The author enjoys spending time with his family along the coast and eagerly awaits the day when his sons will start pulling in crabs.

safely return these frightening looking creatures was a rush; one that, even today, many adults enjoy but won't confess to.

The beauty of recreational crabbing is the family unity it promotes and the fine-tasting meat it yields. The liberal regulations surrounding this fishery makes it a relaxing pastime, one that can be enjoyed no matter what your age or gender.

The values ingrained within me through crabbing at a young age are still with me today. Kazden, it is my hope that you will endeavor to seek and enjoy crabs as your family has over the generations. I look forward to pulling many crab pots with you and your brother, and of course, those fun family feasts that follow.

Here's to a lifetime of good crabbing.
—Love Dad

Published in 2003 by
Frank Amato Publications, Inc.
PO Box 82112 • Portland, Oregon 97282 • (503) 653-8108
Softbound ISBN: 1-57188-288-X • Softbound UPC: 0-81127-00109-5

Photography by Scott Haugen
Illustration on page 12 by Tony Appert
Book Design: Tony Amato
Printed in Hong Kong

3 5 7 9 10 8 6 4

Contents

ACKNOWLEDGMENTS

Attaining local knowledge from marina personnel can enhance one's knowledge about crabbing in the area and is a wonderful way to meet interesting folks.

I would like to thank the many people who made this book possible. From marine biologists to old-timers carrying a wealth of crabbing experience beneath their belt, were it not for your insight, many of the accounts within this book would not have come to fruition.

As in other sport-fishing circles, crabbing connects us with people who desire similar experiences. Regardless of when you initiate your crabbing career, there's always someone out there willing to offer advice and set you on your way. Meeting such people, learning from them and putting to practice their advice is part of what makes crabbing so appealing.

Many recreational crabbers don't live near the coast, and can only make it to the bays on weekends and holidays. At these times, many locals are called upon for their advice and wisdom, and to them we should be thankful. It's the people who are in the trenches month after month, even when the crabbing is poor, who truly educate others about recreational crabbing. From resident crabbers to tackle-shop owners and ardent weekend warriors, you are the ones who keep this sport going and who should be proud of what you've done to encourage and promote the joys to be had through recreational crabbing.

For the many friends and family members who assisted in the compilation of materials needed for this book, I thank you. Special thanks goes to my parents, Jerry and Jean Haugen and my wife Tiffany, for their extended support and encouragement. Such a unique book could not have been produced without their assistance. I would also like to thank our Creator for supplying such a unique creature to pursue, both in sport and fare.

INTRODUCTION

One of the greatest aspects of recreational crabbing is the family unity it promotes. Here, Jason, Sandra and Bailee Reed enjoy a fine day on the bay.

Few marine-related pastimes promote family togetherness like recreational crabbing. Of the many crab species found along the Pacific Coast, the Dungeness crab is by far the most sought after, most delectable member of the crustacean family. From Alaska to Mexico, Dungeness crabs are pursued for sport and their fine eating quality.

To my knowledge this is the first book solely dedicated to the how-to aspects encompassing recreational Dungeness crabbing. There are books out there that touch on crabbing, in addition to the quest for clams and other creatures of the sea, but the comprehensive insight found within these pages makes this a unique work.

The intention of this book is to serve the needs of budding crabbers; those looking to delve into the sport on an independent level, with friends or as an entire family unit. Additionally, there is infor-

mation within these pages that will likely benefit even seasoned crabbers, making for an extensive work that will, to some degree, educate people no matter what their level of crabbing experience.

By taking a close look at the lifestyle of the Dungeness crab, the many ways in which they can be pursued, where to search for them and how to prepare them, this book will allow people to build a solid crabbing foundation. In addition, some of the information found in these pages may open up new avenues to the crabbing world, something you may not have even considered doing when it comes to pursuing crabs. Have you ever thought of diving for crabs, or tossing your pots offshore, or raking crabs while wading through tiny pools on a minus tide? These are just a few of the topics to be highlighted in *Recreational Dungeness Crabbing*.

Crabbing can be done near a number of prime family vacation sites, and planning such trips can be half the fun.

As a former high school science teacher—now a full-time writer—with a lifelong interest and level of involvement in the outdoors, I feel uniquely qualified to compile a book such as this. The ultimate purpose of this work is to educate and encourage people to get out there and experience, firsthand, what crabbing is all about.

For thousands of years, people have been drawn to the coast of the Pacific Northwest in search of food. The cool, clean waters of the Pacific Ocean supplied many Native Americans with valued food before the first white man set foot on the continent. Explorers also learned of the many riches to be found in our sea. Today, Dungeness crabs are among the most popular items on restaurant menus from Alaska to California. The coastal communities along Washington and Oregon largely depend on crabs as a source of recreational income, be it through active

crabbing or those seeking a prepared meal in a restaurant.

While many of the how-to aspects of this book can be applied virtually anywhere Dungeness crabs are accessible to sportsmen, the regional focus will be held to portions of the Oregon and Washington Coast, where the bulk of recreational crabbing is carried out. If further where-to information is desired, either within Oregon, Washington, California, Alaska or British Columbia, it can be attained by contacting respective regional fish and wildlife offices within those areas.

Involving the family in the planning process, from beginning to end, is something that should not be overlooked when endeavoring to take up this fine sport. Safety checks can be taught to youngsters, gear properly evaluated as a family team and even natural history lessons can be taught. Take the time and opportunity to educate youngsters on what they might see

Matt Haugen educates his son Drew on one of the many responsibilities surrounding crabbing. With crabs being so plentiful, capturing the attention of young minds is easy.

*Be on the lookout for marauding seals and sea lions who can strip baits
from crab rings and ruin an otherwise good day on the water.*

while crabbing. Killer whales may be observed in a bay, frolicking sea lions near the boat and an array of aquatic life near docks and even in your pots. There are also great opportunities to explore tide pools while at the coast. The bird life is far different from what's seen inland and noting their adaptations which allow them to survive in a coastal habitat is intriguing to young minds.

The information found in this book is not a supplement to, nor a para-phrased version of state-specific sport fishing regulations, and should not be relied upon as such. Shellfish regula-tions are forever changing, and prior to heading to the water, sportsmen must be familiar with the rules and regula-tions in the specific area they intend on visiting. Being aware of present regula-tions and regulatory changes will not only assure crabbing practices are held within legal means, but that a more enjoyable time can be had by all partic-ipants.

By taking an interest in the cumula-tive aspects surrounding crabbing, the chances of developing the minds of youngsters and rooting in them an appreciation for the sport and the envi-ronment, increases the likelihood for them to bond with such a matchless sport. Only through experience can a complete appreciation of sport crabbing be realized, which is why I encourage people to get on the water as often as possible.

*Youngsters are intrigued with crabs,
no matter what the size.*

CHAPTER 1

NATURAL HISTORY

To fully understand and appreciate the Dungeness crab, we must take a look at its amazing life cycle, where it lives, and its habits. By knowing such information, not only will a more complete knowledge be developed toward the sport of crabbing and what it takes to preserve it, but increased harvest success rates may also result.

Consider a big-game hunter; the

This hard-shelled, adult male Dungeness crab is what you're after. Note the colors and barnacles on this old boy.

The underside of an exceptional male Dungeness crab. The dark coloration indicates his advanced stage of development.

Compound eyes set atop movable stalks constitute a crab's sense of sight.

more this person knows about the animal they pursue, the better their chances of success. Crabbing is no different. The more that can be learned about the Dungeness crab, the better the odds of filling your limit quota. This knowledge also carries over into the preservation of this fishery for future generations, and develops within, an understanding of how to properly and effectively use sport crabbing as a tool of conservation by keeping populations in check.

The Dungeness crab (*Cancer magister*) derives its name from a shallow bay inside Dungeness Spit, along the south shore of the Straits of Juan de Fuca, and the small fishing village of Dungeness. This crab has a wide distribution, stretching from Alaska's Cook Inlet as far south as Magdalena Bay, Mexico.

Dungeness crabs are crustaceans, relatives of the lobster and shrimp, that feature jointed bodies and appendages. Four pairs of walking legs and a set of pincers, along with two compound, stalked eyes and a pair of antennae, give this creature a prehistoric appearance. The broad, chitinous shell of the Dungeness crab is purple to orangish-brown in color and this exoskeleton serves as its sole support system.

Reproduction

Dungeness crabs will commence mating in the spring, though the ritual may carry over well into fall. Male crabs are polygamous, and when in their hard-shelled phase will mate with multiple soft-shelled, or newly molted females. Because only male crabs can be harvested, both in sport and commercial fisheries, understanding the crab's reproductive cycle is vital to accurately monitor their overall harvest.

Mating occurs near shore, outside of estuaries. During the time of copulation, the female crab stores the sperm in a receptacle. This receptacle is shed with each molt, explaining why she cannot mate at any other time except following a molt. When the eggs are fully developed they are laid, or extruded, to the underside of her abdomen, where they are carried until hatching. A mature female can carry as many as 2.5 million eggs. This cluster of eggs is commonly referred to as the "sponge." Fertilization takes place during the egg-laying stage.

Females carrying their eggs often retreat to subtidal zones where they bury themselves in the sand. If, while crabbing, you come across any females carrying a sponge, or a coupled pair of crabs, do your best to keep the level of disruption to a minimum, promptly returning them to the sea.

When the sponge first adheres to the female, it is bright orange in color. As the developing eggs mature, they turn brown prior to hatching. Once hatched, the tiny crabs—in no way resembling adults—swim freely away from their mother and become planktonic. Larval development takes anywhere from four months to as long as a year in northern waters.

The mouth parts of crabs look like something from prehistoric times, though they serve their purpose well.

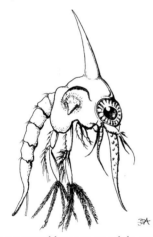

Bearing no resemblance to an adult, crabs in the zoea stage drift out from ashore, living off plankton.

Before the crab molts into its first juvenile stage, it undergoes a succession of six stages; five zoea in which they look nothing whatsoever like a crab, and one megalopa form, where they more closely resemble a shrimp than a crab. As the larvae break free of their egg membrane, development of their spines takes place, deterring attacks by predators. During the megalope stage, the shrimp-like crabs use their mavillipeds to help move their 1/4-inch-long bodies.

The Molt

Approximately a year after mating occurs, the young crabs finally bear a resemblance to their species and adopt a lifestyle centering around the bottom of the ocean. Due to their hard exoskeleton, shells are shed, or molted, with each growth stage. Molting takes place approximately seven times during a crab's first year of living on the bottom. As a crab ages, its molting markedly decelerates. One year after adopting a

A half-inch in size, this young crab recently adopted a bottom-dwelling lifestyle.

A dead crab? Look closely before reporting mass "die-offs" to local authorities. Closer inspection shows this to be nothing more than a molted shell.

Molting crabs literally back out of their shells, leaving behind even their gill coverings and eye stalks.

benthonic lifestyle, a crab will grow from 1/4 inch in shell width, up to 1 3/4 inches across the carapace. After two years of bottom life, the crab will be four inches across the back, and at three years, 5 3/4 inches. The growth stage between molts, referred to as an instar, is at fairly similar rates between both sexes during the first two years.

After two years, the female's growth rate slows when compared to a male's. Only a small percentage of adult females will exceed 6 1/4 inches across the back, while males can exceed 10 inches and weigh in excess of three pounds. A male crab can increase the width of his carapace by one inch and his weight by as much as 65% during a single molt. This is why you often hear of crabbers desiring hard-shelled, full crabs.

At two years of age, sexual maturity can be reached in Dungeness crabs. Male crabs often sexually mature at least a year prior to reaching legal harvest size, assuring the perpetuation of the species. Under ideal conditions, Dungeness crabs can live eight to ten

years, with some reportedly living as long as 13 years.

Prior to molting its exterior shell, a soft, flexible new shell has developed underneath. During the act of molting, the old shell separates across the rear of the crab, along what's known as the suture line. Once the suture line has split open, the crab can literally back out of its old shell, legs and all. Surprisingly, even the eye stalk coverings and gill tissues remain with the shed exoskeleton. During minus tides, and in areas where waves have carried them to the beach, these shed skeletons are often mistaken for dead crabs. In calm conditions, the carapace may even fall into place, giving the illusion of a healthy, dead crab. Fish and wildlife agencies field hundreds of such reports on these false fatalities throughout the year, so be sure and check the specimens closely prior to reporting any form of mass die-off.

After molting, crabs often spend the next few days buried in the sand, hidden from predators. Because their tissues are saturated with water that expands the shell, freshly molted crabs are susceptible

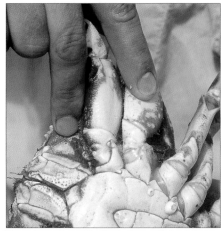

Checking a crab for firmness can be done by applying pressure on the body beneath the pincer, or by gently squeezing the upper portion of a walking leg.

to harsh environmental conditions and predation. If you come across a soft-shelled specimen in your pot, take extra caution to return it safely to the sea. A truly softshelled crab appears greenish across the back and has clean, white legs. It's easy to recognize a softshell crab by touch. If you have a crab in question, turn it on its back and gently press the body, beneath the cheliped. You can also detect shell softness by squeezing the largest segment of any walking leg. If there is any give in either of these spots, the crab is too soft-shelled and won't be full of meat. Softshell crabs should be carefully returned to the sea so

This crab was lucky to survive the loss of a claw, regenerating a new one.

RECREATIONAL DUNGENESS CRABBING

they can fully develop. In Washington, possessing softshell crabs carries a healthy fine. (It will take about two months for a molted crab to become hard-shelled and filled with meat.)

Studies show that crabs have the ability to regenerate lost appendages, but the process impedes their overall survival rate. A study done in Washington revealed that up to 42% of crabs die after losing legs; some by simply bleeding to death. To completely regenerate a severed appendage takes up to three molts, which explains why small, misshapen pincers may be found on some crabs. If an old crab loses a claw, it could take years to regenerate, as their molting rate considerably declines. Noting this, take extra care when removing undersized males and all female crabs from the pot. If they've clamped on to a string, wire, or any part of the trap, don't attempt to force them free. Pulling against their strong, vice-like grip will likely result in dismemberment. Instead, let go, allow the crab time to relax then remove them from the trap or ring.

The author with a pot full of crabs on a gorgeous day at the coast.

Habits, Diet & When to Crab

Dungeness crabs are widely distributed throughout their subtidal zones and prefer living in sandy or muddy bottomed saltwater habitat. They also thrive in environments where eel grass is plentiful, affording good cover and ideal hunting conditions. Dungeness crabs are capable of tolerating changes in salinity levels, which explains why they can also be found in estuaries. Typically inhabiting depths of no greater than 90 feet they have been found 600 feet beneath the surface, but recreational crabbers normally pursue crabs in 15 to 75 feet of water.

The feeding habits of Dungeness crabs coincide with tidal fluctuations. During extreme tidal changes, crabs will bury themselves in the sand to prevent being carried away by the current. When feeding, crabs hunt along the sea floor in search of prey, or patiently await for prey to pass by. Relying on a heightened sense of smell to locate food, crabs are carnivorous and will scavenge when opportunities arise. Their diet includes, but is not limited to, clams, shrimp, mussels, small crabs—of even their own kind—worms, squid, snails and eggs from crabs and fish. They will also forage on dead organisms, including fish, though they will shy away from rotting, putrid flesh.

Knowing when crabs are apt to feed dictates when crabbers should be most active. Because bays are influenced by tidal changes, so too are the feeding times of crabs. Crabs are most active during the peak of high (flood) and low (ebb) tides. These slack tides, as they are

The uncertainty and intrigue of crabbing is what makes it so addictive, no matter what your age.

crabs are full of meat and their shells firm. But this is not the only reason why crabbing is productive during these months. Rainfall and the intrusion of fresh water into bays can also influence crabbing productivity, which is why crabbing can be slow during rainy months or spring months when mountain snows are melting and feeding into bays.

Because crabs prefer water that is high in salinity, the closer you can set your pots to the mouth of a bay, generally, the better the crabbing will be. If crabbing from a boat is not an option, search for large bays that have generous tidal changes, where crabs are more apt to actively feed farther up the bay. Shore-bound crabbers can also seek out docks and piers that allow crabbing closer to the mouth of a bay, where salinity levels run higher. Not all bays have a large movement of salt water entering them during an incoming tide, and knowing this can impact when and where in the bay you decide to crab. For example, crabbing high in a bay that sees minimal tidal movement is not the best choice. Your best bet here is to get as low in the bay as possible, preferably near the mouth, where salinity levels run higher and crabs are more likely to be found.

During months of low rainfall, crabbing can also be good. There's an old adage that "the 'ber months are best for crabbing." This translates into the months ending in 'ber as being ideal. While September and October are likely the two best crabbing months, if conditions are right, the action can carryover well into January. I recall years when crabbing has been productive into March, thanks to low levels of rainfall, thus lesser amounts of fresh water making its way into bays. The months of July and August can also be good for crabbing. Molts can also vary from

called, are when current flow is at a minimum, and when crabbers want to have their gear in the water. Though hitting both slacks are good, a slack flood is better than a slack ebb due to the increased salinity levels which keep crabs more active.

Crabbing can also be highly productive when differences between tidal changes are minimal, where the exchange between high and low tide are narrow. If you're looking to maximize your crabbing time on the water, try selecting days when there is a low high tide, and a high low tide. In such conditions, the crabbing can be very good for up to 12 consecutive hours. But if you're not able to hit such tides, the best time to be on the water is one hour prior to, and following, a high or a low tide.

As for the best time of year to crab, it's usually in late summer and fall, when

The massive claws of red crabs have been known to break the fingers of humans, so handle with extreme caution.

region to region, even within regions, meaning crabbing should not be left solely to the 'ber months.

If, when crabbing, you are catching only female crabs, try relocating your pots a couple hundred yards away. Crabs will move about in groups called migration clusters. Males and females travel in separate groups from one another, typically moving into shallower waters the first half of the year. Documentation on tagged Dungeness crabs reveals they can travel more than 75 miles with their active lifestyle.

Red rock crabs have unique coloration and liberal harvest laws apply throughout much of their range.

The Red Rock Crab

A close cousin to the Dungeness, the red or red rock crab (*Cancer productus*) gets its name from both its physical coloration and the habitat in which it thrives. The red crab rarely exceeds six inches in shell width and does not contain the meaty volume Dungeness crabs possess. The meat however, is flavorful, and as these crabs don't count toward your Dungeness daily catch limits, they are worth taking home.

Red rock crabs can be distinguished by their red carapace and large, over-sized, black-tipped pincers. Their shell width is considerably wider than it is long, giving this crab a narrower appearance than the Dungeness.

Where their population densities run high, red crabs can have a noticeable impact on oyster and hard-shell clam populations. They prefer a rocky habitat, which explains why many of these crabs are harvested off docks and near jettys.

Size restrictions and catch limits on both Dungeness and red crabs vary from state to state, even within states, and will be addressed in respective chapters.

CHAPTER 2

GEARING UP

An attractive aspect of recreational crabbing is the minimal gear that's required. If you don't wish to invest in crab pots or rings, they can often be rented at virtually every bay where crabbing opportunities exist. Boats can also be rented and baits bought, making for a simple, hassle-free experience.

But if you're serious about crabbing and wish to partake in the sport more than once or twice a year, investing in the proper gear will be to your advantage. Before heading afield, however, check local crabbing regulations in the area you plan on hitting. During periods of high molting occurrence, some bays may restrict the use of certain types of gear. Other factors may also cause temporary regulatory changes that anglers are responsible for keeping abreast of.

Crab Rings

The most widely-used crab-catching device is the crab ring, or ring-trap. The crab ring consists of two metal hoops, joined by mesh webbing. The larger, upper hoop ranges from 24 to 32 inches across, while the bottom, lower hoop is about a foot in diameter. A rope affixes to three points on the upper ring, assuring that a balanced pull is had during the retrieval process.

When placed in the water, crab rings lay flat, allowing crabs to come and go as they please. For this reason, it's imperative these rings be checked every 10 to 15 minutes. Not only should rings be pulled often to avoid loss of keeper crabs, but the baits will regularly need to be checked. Seals and other ocean life

Securing bait in the center of a crab ring ensures it will evenly settle on the bottom. A wide-hooped ring will also increase the odds of catching more crabs.

can wreak havoc on baits in these exposed rings, rendering them useless.

When used in the bay from a boat, highly visible floats must be fixed to the ropes. Washington requires your name and address be clearly written on red-and-white buoys in permanent marker. If crabbing from docks, buoys need not be attached, as you are tying directly to the dock.

In baiting a crab ring, be sure to securely place the bait in the center of the bottom ring, so the ring settles flush on the bottom. When pulling a crab ring, do so as quickly as possible. The idea is to swiftly lift the upper ring to prevent crabs from crawling out and to create enough force by the water pushing against the crabs, that their movement will be restricted. Keep pulling hard until the entire ring is clear of the water surface.

The use of crab rings are legal for year-round use in all waters, except in the offshore ocean waters of Oregon, where fall closures on Dungeness crabs prevail.

Slip Rings

These nifty devices would be classified somewhere between a crab ring and a crab pot. Two sturdy rings are separated by fixed bars, with a collapsible mesh body fitting between them. When in a relaxed state on the bottom, the mesh body lays flat, allowing for the entry of crabs into the framed structure. The drawback, as with rings, is that crabs are free to come and go. But the advantage is that once you start hoisting a ring trap, the mesh sides that are attached to the mainline instantly raise tight against the uppermost ring, assuring no crabs escape.

Slip rings are ideal if working deep sections of water, where keeping a fast, steady pull on open rings is difficult. Crabs are also simple to remove from slip rings, thanks to the collapsible sides.

Star Traps

These three-sided, pyramid style traps are handy for crabbing off docks and in calm bays. Their light weight makes them easy to pull, and the fact they fold up flat allows for easy storage of multiple traps.

Once on the bottom of the ocean, star traps lay flat. A rope system connects all three sides of this trap, and combined with a spring-loaded hinge system, allows for a quick-closing

Slip rings offer crabs easy access, but take on the properties of a pot once the retrieval begins.

action once the retrieval process begins. A quick jerking action makes certain all three sides of this trap spring shut at once, seizing all crabs within.

Crab Pots

Crab pots come in various shapes and sizes, from round to square to rectangular. Many people prefer round pots over more linear styles because crabs are more likely to work their way around a circle than along straight lines with 90° turns.

Crab pots are ideal for three reasons: they keep seals and other scavengers away from your bait, they don't have to be checked as often, and they prevent keeper-size crabs from escaping. They can also be left overnight in many crabbing waters.

Note that crab pots must feature an escape route for undersized crabs. The top, side, or parts of one section of the trap must be tethered shut by a material that can rot away in a short period of

time. A 100% natural cotton cord or other fast-rotting fiber will ensure crabs have a way of escaping the pots should they become lost at sea.

Collapsible crab traps are one of the greatest innovations to hit the market. These inexpensive, square traps are easy to use, light weight, take up minimal storage space and keep bait-robbing intruders at bay. They work just like a pot, with hinged doors that swing open to the inside, holding any large crabs that enter. Bait can be wired directly to the top or bottom of the trap, or placed in bait boxes.

Removing crabs from a collapsible trap is simple and can be done by opening one of the sides, allowing easy access. But don't remove all the crabs before tossing this, or any other freshly baited trap overboard. Leave a couple small crabs in the pot, as the noise they make while feeding is believed to attract larger crabs. The impact of these smaller crabs on your bait is minimal.

Round crab pots, versus square ones, are the choice of many serious crabbers.

In addition to being attracted by the smell of bait and the sound of other feeding crabs, light will lure crabs into a pot. Knowing this, attaching a glow stick inside your trap can yield surprising results. I've used

In the event your pots are lost at sea, they must be equipped with a way for captive crabs to escape. A cotton cord rots away in a matter of days, creating a large escape route. Check local laws for specifics.

Leaving 2 or 3 small crabs in a pot when dropping it back in the ocean is a ploy to attract more crabs. The noises of their feeding antics will capture the attention of nearby crabs, luring them in.

RECREATIONAL DUNGENESS CRABBING

Suspended from the top of a pot, glow sticks give off light that attracts crabs.

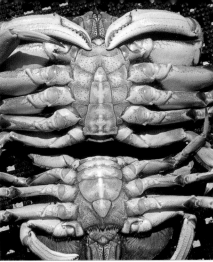

glow sticks enough to honestly believe they make a difference in attracting crabs.

The steep, triangular shape of the male Dungeness crab's abdomen (top) is easy to distinguish from the more rounded female (bottom).

Sexing & Measuring

Only male Dungeness crabs can be retained by both commercial and recreational sportsmen. Males are distinguished from females by their narrow abdomen. The abdomens of females are distinctly wider and are more rounded, leaving little question as to their sex.

In Washington and Oregon, both sexes of red rock crabs can be harvested. While there are no size restrictions on

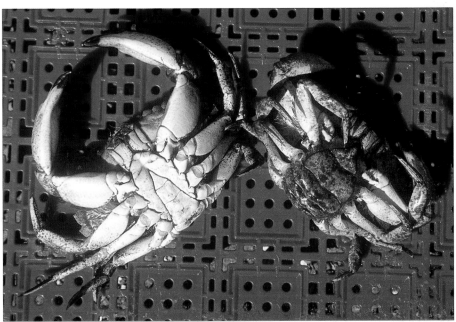

Male (left) and female red rock crabs have distinct abdomens. Laws regarding the take of these crabs are different than those of the Dungeness; consult local regulations prior to heading out.

red rock crabs taken in Oregon, Washington requires a minimum of 5 inches. Once aboard, it's imperative crabs are accurately measured to verify they fit within the legal requirements established by state fish and wildlife agencies.

Dungeness crabs in Oregon carry a statewide 5 3/4 inches minimal size limit, while Washington regulations vary from 5 3/4 inches to 6 1/4 inches. Prior to heading afield, be certain to check minimum size requirements and daily bag limits for the specific regions you intend on working.

The most accurate measurements of crabs are taken with commercially available calipers. These fixed, plastic gauges leave no room for error, unlike many homemade models I've seen. Given their low cost and propensity to break during the frantic times when a pot full of crabs is hoisted aboard, it's not a bad idea to have two or three of these calipers on hand.

When measuring a crab, the reading is taken from the widest part of the carapace, across the crab's back. Slide the calipers into the slots of the shell, just behind the rearmost point or tips. If the fit is tight, matching or exceeding the minimum requirement notched in the calipers for the body of water in which you're crabbing, you have a keeper.

Handling Crabs

Once you have a crab in the pot—be it a keeper or a throwback—safe and efficient removal is important; not only for the crab's sake, but yours as well. When removing crabs from a pot or ring, it's best done by slipping a thumb beneath the abdomen from behind, while placing the four fingers atop the carapace. This keeps the fingers away from the pincers and the thumb in an impossible spot to reach.

If a crab is facing you, and it's difficult to work a hand around to the backside, it can be grabbed, front-on. The key here is making sure both pincers are

A proper measuring device is imperative when on the water.

RECREATIONAL DUNGENESS CRABBING

Pinning both claws of a crab against the body (left) is a safe way to handle them, as is placing a thumb on the abdomen and forefingers on the carapace.

being held tight against the crab's body. If this is the case, firmly press a thumb on its back, with the cup of the hand covering the eyes. At the same time the thumb comes in contact with the carapace, the four fingers will pin the pincers against the body, immobilizing the weapons.

Grabbed in one of these two ways, the pincers will not be able to reach any fingers. Don't panic at the sharp walking legs as they prick your hand, this is normal and harmless. In addition, try and refrain from toting crabs by the legs, for not only may they become dismembered, they might nab a finger with those nasty pincers.

With a solid hold, place the crab on its back, on a flat surface. When on its back, a crab is incapacitated and less stressed. This will allow you to gather the crabs for measuring, while quickly returning the non-keepers. I've had up to a dozen crabs laying on the bottom of the boat this way; as long as they can't reach anything that will allow them leverage to flip over, they stay put.

Incidental Gear

Once on the water, especially if operating from a boat, the more prepared you are to deal with quick repair jobs, the better. In addition to the standard gear required for boaters, found in all crabbers' goody-bags should be a pair of wire cutters, wire, bungies and heavy string. Given all the metal parts existing on crab pots, there's no telling when pliers will come in handy. An extra spool of wire or a bungy assures the quick repair of pots, both along the metal frames and wire bodies, while a heavy-gauge string allows for mending crab rings and the sides of star traps.

Needlenose pliers are also handy for crabs that do get ahold of a finger. It's virtually impossible to pry these claws with a human hand, and the aid of pliers can be invaluable. I once had a crab latch on to my finger and two of us could not work it from the death-grip. My buddy grabbed a pair of needlenose pliers and gently lifted the upper claw, allowing me to slip my bloody finger from the grasp. Crab claws can break human fingers, especially red crabs, and their power should not be underestimated.

When pulling pots, wearing gloves is wise. Not only do gloves protect the hands from harsh salt water, they afford a better grip on the ropes. Rubber, neoprene, and synthetic gloves all serve their purpose well.

Each pot and ring should be assembled with at least 50 feet of rope, though I prefer 75 feet of rope in case I decide to hit deep waters or head offshore. Some crabbers won't use anything less than 100 feet of rope, to accommodate severe tidal fluctuations. Regardless of the length of rope you choose, keeping a couple hundred feet of extra rope on board is not a bad idea. In addition to being able to quickly rig deeper-running

When removing crabs from the pot, placing them on their back ensures they remain immobile.

pots, you may find the rope handy in towing stranded boats or to solve a

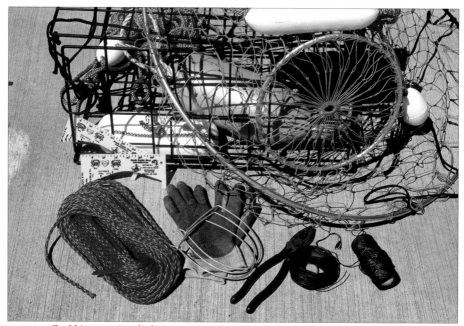

Crabbing requires little excess gear, but what's shown here can come in handy.

variety of unforeseen events that may arise. It should be pointed out, a thicker diameter rope attached to each pot is much easier to pull than thinner ones, and is worth the few extra dollars for what it saves on your hands at the end of a long day of yanking pots.

The more prepared you are before taking to the water, the more enjoyable the overall crabbing experience will be. And remember, no matter when or where you go, think safety first.

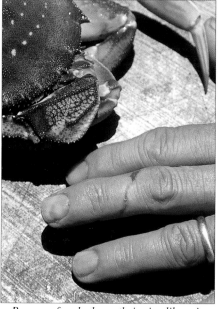

Beware of crab claws, their vice-like grip will draw blood. Having a pair of pliers within reach at all times is a good idea, as human fingers are not strong enough to pry the pincers apart.

The thicker the rope (right), the more comfortable pulling in your pots will be. This can be especially important if running in deep water, or if pulling numerous pots during the day.

CHAPTER 3

THE RIGHT BAIT

Crabs rely on a heightened sense of smell to detect food; something the recreational crabber needs to consider when selecting baits. The more scent your bait disperses into the water, the better the odds of catching crabs. A key element not to be taken for granted when crabbing is the bait. Bait can make or break a trip, and selecting the best bait available is important for maximizing success.

Catching your own bait has to be considered one of the more joyous responsibilities of crabbing. While bait can be purchased at local marinas where crabbing occurs, there's nothing like gathering your own bait throughout the

Natural prey of the crab, clams are one of the better bait choices. Simply break the shells to release scent and place in a bait box.

Sport fishing for shad is one of the most enjoyable responsibilities of crabbing, and yields the best bait.

course of the year, anticipating the time when it will finally be put to use.

There are several baits crabs find attractive, but some work better than others. The golden rule to follow when selecting and gathering your baits is, it must be fresh. Of course, freezing your bait is okay, and is often the only option, but you'll find that freezer-burned baits will definitely be outfished by fresh or freshly-frozen baits.

Laboratory observations have shot down the old theory that crabs prefer rotting, putrid flesh. In fact, just the contrary is true; crabs will avoid decayed flesh, preferring fresh meat as their mainstay.

The Top Three Baits

Many crabbers claim clams to be the number-one bait choice for enticing crabs. Seeing as how crabs live on the bottom and routinely forage on clams, this only makes sense. Used fresh or frozen, clams can be placed in a bait box or bait bag and fastened to the pot. Breaking the clams' shells open, allowing the scents to escape, is a good idea. Because digging clams requires a great deal of effort, some people may find it hard to part with their catch, opting instead to use other baits.

Shad are a preferred bait, and are what I consider to be the ultimate crab attractor. Shad, the largest member of the herring family, carry pungent oils that drive crabs wild. On several occasions I've tossed a pot baited with shad next to one baited with salmon, clams and other bait selections. In every instance, the shad outfished the other baits. In fact, on one pull, the trap baited

Shad is regarded as the premier crab bait. The author has experimented with many baits, and agrees shad is the most productive of all.

with a fresh salmon carcass caught the day before yielded only one large female crab, while the pot right next to it, baited with a whole shad, produced 26 crabs, including seven legal males.

Shad are a thrilling fish to catch, pound-for-pound being one of the scrappiest fighters around. Their spring and early-summer runs come at a good time, when crabbing is just getting started. Due to their high oil content, shad also keep very well in the freezer. If caught in the spring, there is no problem keeping them frozen until late fall and into winter. When the fishing is good, upwards of 100 shad can be caught in a single outing, meaning the big challenge might be finding ample freezer space to store so much bait. The fact that shad is the only bait I've had stolen from my pots by unscrupulous crabbers attests to its effectiveness as a premier crab bait.

Salmon and steelhead carcasses—as well as those from bottomfish—are also one of the best attractants for luring in crabs. The key here is using the whole, filleted carcass, not just the heads. While fish heads will work, they don't contain the meaty content found on an entire fish skeleton, thus they'll perform below par. The more flesh these crabs have to chew on, the more scent will be released into the water, increasing the number of crabs that will ultimately seek out the bait.

If you catch a high number of salmon and steelhead, it's worth cutting off the fins and tails to use as crab bait. The fatty tissue contained at the base of the fins make them ideal baits, and when placed in a bait bag, they are very effective. If you don't do much salmon fishing, their carcasses can often be obtained at public marinas, where fish-cleaning stations are in place. I've also acquired fresh tuna carcasses this way, which also serve as very effective bait.

Salmon and steelhead make good crab bait, though filleted carcasses are preferred over just the heads.

Other Bait Options

Turkey and chicken parts are popular baits; legs, necks and backs being preferred. These parts of the poultry contain fatty oils that release a great deal of scent into the water, something crabs find appealing. Attaching a frozen turkey leg to the pot can be very fruitful, as the thawing process slowly releases the fat, greatly extending the timeframe over which this bait will produce.

Crushing raw chicken and turkey parts, and combining them with ground fish, has also been proven to produce crabs on a regular basis. The oils of these birds serve as scent carriers to transport the smell of the fish over a wider area. Because these bird oils are hydrophobic, they will greatly extend the life of any bait, increasing their level of "catchability."

Beef is also an established crab bait. Fatty parts of the meat, bones containing meat scraps and fat, along with sinuous tissues, all work well.

Along the Oregon coast, seals and sea lions are notorious for robbing crab rings of their bait. Mink carcasses can often be purchased at various marinas along the coast, where they serve well as crab bait, while at the same time fending off sea mammals. These mink are supplied by a mink rancher near Mount Angel, Oregon, who trucks the skinned, frozen corpses to marinas. Due to the demand of mink for bait, and their limited supply, they may not always be available for use, but crabbers who use them on a regular basis consider them the best bait going.

Artificial baits are also known to produce crabs, and can serve as an effective alternative bait or to enhance your natural bait selection. The Catcher Company, makers of Smelly Jelly, produces a Crab Attractant bait carrying an extra-strong scent that

Mink are a super bait, especially when working areas high in seal numbers as these marine mammals will avoid them.

RECREATIONAL DUNGENESS CRABBING

Artificial baits, like Smelly Jelly Crab Attractant, have proven effective for many crabbers.

appeals to crabs. This bait can be applied to existing baits or used alone. When complementing other baits, spreading Crab Attractant on the bait itself, and on parts of the crab pot, can considerably enhance your set. When used alone, spread Crab Attractant on parts of the trap, or better yet in a nylon stocking. As the Crab Attractant lathers up, it soaks into the stocking, prolonging the rate at which scent is dispersed. This is a great way of extending the life of your bait, as when the flesh may be eaten away, the allure of the Crab Attractant hangs on. I've also talked with people who've had good success placing a generous portion of Crab Attractant in a small yogurt container poked with holes, inside a bait box, or clipped directly to the trap.

Affixing Baits

There are several ways to affix baits to your rings and traps. The most important factor to be sure of is that the bait is secure, so as not to float around or be carried away from your set by crabs or currents. Securely centering the bait in the trap ensures the device will set

Suspending bait from the top of a pot not only optimizes scent dispersal, it makes crabs work for their meal.

A mesh bag is preferred by many crab fans who feel the device makes the bait accessible while extending its longevity.

to the top of the trap. This is best done with a bungy or tie. Simply place a bungy hook or tie-off to the top of the bag/box. Lift snugly, securing it to the top of the pot. This will suspend the bait preventing it from being sanded in and keeping crabs from congregating outside the top of the pot, which often happens to baits placed tight against the top.

If using clams, small fish parts, ground baits and other loose rations for bait, placing them in a bait box or bait bag is the ticket. These bait-holding contraptions prevent crabs from devouring all the contents, meaning the baits will not have to be replaced as often as exposed baits.

Nylon, mesh bait bags are preferred by some crabbers, as they fit and hold the bait selection nicely. These mesh bait bags also allow the bait to be more accessible to crabs, keeping their interest level high. Mesh bags are good choices to use in ring and star traps, where keeping the optimal number of crabs on the bait is the objective. Contrary to popular belief, crabs will not slice through these bags, or the netting on your rings for that matter; their claws are made for crushing, not cutting.

A final method of securing your bait that I've found effective is to take a two-inch-wide, 12-inch-long section of PVC pipe and drill several holes in it. Cap both ends, one of which can be removed. Place your cut-up baits in the tube, wire it to the pot and you're set. These tubes are popular in the Texas Gulf for attracting sharks, but serve well to keep baits active in crab traps for extended periods, as the crabs can't consume the bait. Some avid crabbers also testify that the white PVC pipe plays on the crabs' sense of sight, attracting them to the pot.

level, allowing for easy access by ravenous crabs.

If using whole shad or filleted fish carcasses, affixing them to the bottom of the crab ring or star trap with a bait clip is a good idea. If using a crab pot or slip-ring set-up, I like fastening the bait to the top of the trap. This position keeps the bait suspended so crabs can't easily devour it, and it also keeps it off the bottom, allowing for a greater dispersal of the scent while preventing sanding-in. Bait clips can be purchased for a nominal fee, and hold up well. Baits can also be wired to the bottom of the trap, but make sure they are snug enough to withstand hungry crabs and powerful current flow, and that the wire is changed regularly.

Another trick is to elevate the top of the bait bag or box by connecting it

No matter what type of bait you choose, or how you go about affixing it to the pot, take the extra time to keep your bait fresh and present it in a way that will most effectively appeal to crabs. Old, washed-out baits that have been picked clean will not be nearly as productive as fresh bait. If in question, change that bait out for a new supply. You've made the effort of heading to the ocean, don't jeopardize your success by skimping on the bait.

There are a variety of methods for securing bait in a pot or ring, and each has its place.

CHAPTER 4

CRABBING FROM A DOCK

One of the major attractions to crabbing is that it can be done from a dock. Simply drive to the beach, find a dock or pier extending into the water, bait, and toss your rings. It's that simple.

But there are steps that can be taken to enhance crabbing success from docks, not the least of which is monitoring tidal movements. While it may be convenient to drive up and drop a ring off a dock, it may not happen to be the best crabbing time.

By consulting tide table books, you can learn precisely when high, low and slack tides will occur, thus maximize your opportunity to catch more crabs. Tide tables contain valuable information for the seagoing sportsman, and crabbers in particular should refer to the complete correction table within this booklet to accurately pinpoint tidal movements and their times of change in the respective area where crabbing activities are planned. On ideal tides,

The ease of tossing a ring on the rig and heading to a port is what makes crabbing from docks so appealing.

Simple steps like reading tide tables can enhance your overall crab catch.

tides, be sure to toss your rings on the side of the dock where the current is flowing away to ensure they don't get carried beneath the dock, becoming entangled in its pilings, and tie them off securely.

Crabbing from moorages and piers, like in all crabbing, is best done during slack tides, when crabs are most active. However, many moorages are protected from fast currents thanks to man-made barriers. This means crabs in protected bays may be active throughout the day.

One misnomer pointed out to me by a veteran crabber, is that it's not necessary to toss your ring as far as humanly possible when crabbing from a dock. Because Dungeness crabs, especially mature males, become territorial as they age, they seek to take up residence in

you may need to arrive at a dock early, to secure the best site from which to crab. If crabbing on incoming or outgoing

Piers are ideal places from which to crab. Typically being positioned closer to the ocean than docks, piers attract good numbers of crabs.

small depressions on the sandy bottom. Pilings supporting moorages and piers help create natural depressions as water moves the sand around them, producing an ideal microenvironment in which crabs thrive.

In fact, crabs have been known to hold tight in these depressions, warding off predators and patiently awaiting food to come their way. I've talked with divers who confirmed this behavior.

Therefore, when crabbing from docks, you can increase your chances of success by dropping the rings straight down, next to a piling. If working an area that allows the use of more than one crabbing ring, it's in your best interest to drop the allotted number of rings next to existing pilings. Don't worry about removing these territorial crabs from their protective domain; once they are gone, others will waste no time claiming their spots.

If moorages or piers extend toward, protrude from, or are surrounded by

When crabbing off docks, drop your pots close to pilings, where depressions in the sand attract territorial males.

RECREATIONAL DUNGENESS CRABBING

A deep, wide-mouthed setup is great for dock crabbing.

rocky structure, the chances of catching red rock crabs escalate. By seeking out such terrain, crabbers can often use the known habitats of these crabs to their advantage, harvesting both red rock and Dungeness crabs from one general location.

Crab rings, ring traps and star traps are the most popular devices used when crabbing from a dock. These units lay flat and feature an exposed bait that will bring crabs in without hesitation. But crabs are also free to come and go in these contraptions. For this reason, it's prudent to yank these devices every 10 to 15 minutes. Frequent checking will result in higher catch rates, verifying your bait is fresh and will allow you to rid the bait of small, undersized crabs.

Inquiring at local marinas as to the best moorages and piers to crab from can pay big dividends. Crabbing off docks is fun and safe for the entire family, and should not be overlooked as a productive means by which to harvest delectable crabs.

CHAPTER 5

CRABBING FROM A BOAT

Having access to a boat greatly enhances the odds of crabbing success, be it in bays or amongst islands. Not only does it afford entry into more waters, it provides a freedom of movement landlocked crabbers don't have.

If you don't own a boat, several marinas along the Pacific Coast rent them out, along with all the amenities needed for a successful day of crabbing. Going in with a few buddies makes renting a craft affordable, especially if you each pull a limit of crabs. The alternative of purchasing pricey crab at the market easily justifies renting a boat for a day on the water.

If you're unfamiliar with operating a boat, yet want to get on the water for crab, guides can be hired. Good friend and veteran guide Bob Cobb of Reedsport, Oregon, routinely takes crabbers into Winchester Bay, though clients here can expect more than just crab.

The best crabbing months, September and October, happen to fall during the peak of the fall chinook salmon run. Cobb offers combination guided trips for salmon and crabs, where crab pots are set on the way out to fish, and are checked on the return trip. Oftentimes, the salmon fishing action takes place near where the pots are

Oregon guide Pat Sullivan (left) offers prime crabbing and fishing excursions. Such combination trips are one of the best deals in which anglers can invest.

Having all your pots baited with ropes wound on top, ready to go, is very efficient when it comes to quickly setting a line.

point. Of course, the number of fellow crabbers occupying the bay may dictate just how spread out your set may be. I've had weekdays where no one was on the water, and weekends where turning the boat around without concern of a collision was impossible.

By dropping your pots in a straight line, not only is running the boat easier, but it allows you to focus your efforts on a single area and to lay a strong scent line. Establishing a row of traps is simple. With your pots baited—ropes and buoys wound and resting atop the pot or inside the rings—prior to reaching your designated crabbing site, simply pick your path of travel and drop the pots as you go. Tossing the pots in level, ropes and all, will allow them to sink straight down, the rope uncoiling as the trap falls.

If you're not having success in this trap line, or find you're catching only females or small crabs, pull the pots and change location. Another approach is to initially set a few traps in different

dropped, meaning they can be frequently checked, freshly baited, and even relocated if necessary. There are guides up and down the coast offering such combination trips, though guided trips focusing exclusively on crabbing can be arranged.

If you have your own boat, pulling a double-duty day on crab and salmon is a thrill. Equipping your pots with plenty of rope and a five-pound weight in each ensures they will "fish" through all tidal changes. A periodic check of the traps allows you to clean them and apply fresh bait. Fishing for salmon during incoming, outgoing and slack tides is ideal, so there's no reason not to have pots out, getting crammed with crabs, while you pursue other ocean cuisine.

When concentrating solely on crabbing from a boat, the objective is to arrange your pots in a workable pattern that fosters efficient operation of the craft. Tossing pots in a straight line, every 15 to 20 yards, is a good starting

Working a line of pots makes for easy, frequent checks and lays a good scent trail.

locations around the bay, pinpointing where the keeper males are lurking. Once a honey hole is located, you may want to move all your traps to that area.

The fewer boats there are on the water at any given time, the more area for you to explore. If you find yourself at a new, unfamiliar bay, don't hesitate asking local crabbers and marine shop owners where they suggest you commence your search for crabs.

If trying to locate precise areas in which to drop pots, depth finders can yield valuable information. These devices are also handy when crabbing in unfamiliar waters. Searching for low spots, where crabs often congregate,

Utilizing a long pole to hook the rope of your pot is not only a good safety feature to have in rough water, but it helps keep ropes from getting too close to propellers.

can be the key to success. Running across water, scanning the bottom until you find a likely looking depth can also save lots of guess work. My buddy, Matt Haugen and I found a sand hole in this way, and turned an otherwise slow day of crabbing into one to remember.

Once a prime crab-producing location has been located, marking it as a waypoint on a GPS or topographical map is a good idea. When such a point is documented, it's easy to return to the exact location, no matter what the tidal conditions. The only concern is that such a locale might become filled in with sand, in which case you simply search for a new location.

Should a GPS not be available, lining up two landmarks may suffice in securing a regular crabbing locale. In one of my favorite bays, the best crabbing lies halfway between a buoy marker and a jetty; no GPS coordinates are needed to find this spot.

When retrieving pots with a boat, utilizing a long pole to hook the buoy line is a good idea. A hooking pole prevents crabbers from leaning and reaching over the edge of the boat, where unsuspecting waves can catch the craft at the wrong time, sending the occupant overboard or into the bottom of the boat. This happens all too often and can be greatly reduced by using a long retrieval pole.

If a weak back or an aging body is keeping you from crabbing in a boat, or if smaller-framed children want to get in on the action, the use of a davit makes bringing in heavy pots a cinch. Attached directly to the boat, this swinging-arm device features a pulley on the end. After hooking the buoy line, thread it through the open-face pulley and hoist away. The effort required to pull heavy pots is greatly reduced with a davit.

RECREATIONAL DUNGENESS CRABBING

Firmly securing two buoys to the end of the rope is a must when crabbing from a boat. Don't skimp on size when it comes to selecting a float. You want floats with enough buoyancy to stay visible in strong currents and high winds. Clearly labeling the buoy with your name and address is a good idea, and is law in the state of Washington. It's also a good idea to attach an ounce of weight to the buoy line, about 10 feet beneath the float. This added weight guards against the line floating to the surface and getting caught in propellers; this too, is law in Washington state.

If crabbing in bays where a strong tidal current is present, use heavy gauge pots or affix a five-pound weight to light-framed pots. The extra weight is wise in these conditions to prevent the pots from being carried to deep waters or even out to sea.

The beauty of running pots from a boat is the extended time that can elapse between check periods. Where legal, pots are often left out overnight. However, if you're serious about quickly securing your limit, frequent checks every 20 minutes or so keeps the bait fresh.

When pulling pots, it's a good idea to wear rubber boots and rain pants. No matter how clear the sky, getting wet is inevitable, and rain pants and the proper footwear can make for a much more comfortable time.

Always pay attention to incoming waves when crabbing from a boat. Sleepers—big waves that make their way past the jaws of an inlet—claim boats every year. When pulling and cleaning pots, it's easy to keep your head down, focused on the task at hand. The captain of the boat should be on a constant lookout for large waves creeping in. If crabbing alone, make sure to

Using a davit, the author's wife, Tiffany Haugen, hoists a load of crabs. This pulley system helps reduce the workload and is popular among crabbers heading out solo.

keep an eye on the progression of incoming waves.

Before returning to the dock—and periodically throughout the day—check beneath floorboards in the boat, any gaps in the vessel, between buckets, gear boxes and fuel tanks for any stray, undersized crabs that may have fallen through a pot. Though it may be unintentional on your part, harboring undersized crabs can, nonetheless, result in a hefty fine.

Taking a few precautions while crabbing from a boat can make all the difference in providing a positive, productive experience. And once you see for yourself how many crabs can be obtained through this technique, you'll become addicted to crabbing for sure.

CHAPTER 6

OFFSHORE CRABBING

One of the best-kept secrets in the recreational crabbing world are the rich, offshore waters that harbor crabs. The sandy environment located just off the main beach and beyond the breakers creates an ideal crab habitat and receives little pressure from sportsmen. When seasons and weather conditions foster access to these sites, the crabbing can be sizzling.

Contrary to popular belief, heading as far as possible offshore is not necessarily the best crabbing option. Sticking close to shore, in 20 to 75 feet

John Cheesman, Captain of Seasports I, yards in an offshore crab pot.

Corrina Wood shows how productive offshore crabbing can be. This one pull yielded more than two dozen crabs, six of which were keepers.

of water where sand accumulates and crabs thrive, will yield high success. Oftentimes you need only travel a couple hundred yards over the bar, or outside the mouth of a bay, to access prime crabbing grounds.

By staying close to shore, typically within 500 yards, rocky outcroppings and deep seas can be avoided. Rock structures claim numerous pots as they get wedged and permanently lodged between them. This is why so many pots and rings are lost by crabbers trying their luck off jettys. In addition, strong currents and deep runs can be

avoided by working closer to shore. Pots tossed too far out are susceptible to being carried away by harsh currents and even large, seagoing vessels. When crabbing offshore, avoid dropping your pots in shipping lanes.

Hitting sandy and muddy bottoms will produce the highest catch of crabs. If you don't have hi-tech sonar to read such features, purchasing a navigational marine map is the way to go. These maps, created by NOAA (National Oceanic Atmospheric Association) can be acquired at local marinas or through the government, and show in great detail what substrates are present along the coastline. Offshore crabbers can use the information on these maps to their advantage, and they are also a safety feature every offshore-going vessel should have on deck.

Though seasonal openings and closures dictate when crabbing beyond bays can be practiced, if you're prepared, the success can be astounding. Not only will these waters yield more crabs, but on average, larger ones as well.

During one of our offshore crabbing quests out of Charleston, Oregon, four of us yanked our limits of crabs in no time, using only eight pots. We were only 300 yards beyond the jetty, crabbing in 30 feet of water where the sandy bottom teamed with crabs.

On another offshore crabbing run out of Winchester Bay, Oregon, we dropped our pots for the day, hammered six salmon, and pulled three limits of crabs on the way back to port. There are marine-licensed guides who can take you on such combination trips, but regardless of who you select, be certain they carry their U.S. Coast Guard Masters License, allowing them to legally operate offshore. July and August are ideal months for these journeys, when the salmon are close to shore and the crabs have harder shells. Guides Pat Sullivan of Sully's Guide Service and Patrick Roelle of Fishpatrick's Guide Service are two men operating off the Oregon Coast who cater to offshore trips for salmon and crab.

Buoy lines stretching 100 feet in length are ideal for offshore crab pots, though if working close to shore, 75 feet of rope will suffice. It's better to have too much rope than not enough, keeping the buoys on the surface. At the same time, adding up to five pounds of extra weight in your pot is a good idea. The added weight will keep the pots on the bottom, guarding against longshore currents that may otherwise carry them away. Be sure to check these pots at least once a day, twice being preferred; you don't want them becoming sanded-in. Those old, barnacle- and kelp-covered buoys that can be seen offshore are a result of commercial crabbers having their large pots covered in sand, something that can be avoided with periodic checks.

Operating from a stable boat is also a must. If the ocean has laid down, accessing offshore waters is not a concern. But if the seas are churning and the bars rough, a sturdy boat is a prerequisite. If the swells are running high and you find yourself in doubt, don't push it, retreat back into the safety of the bay and work for your crabs there.

John Cheesman, Captain of Seasports I Fishing Charters, often takes clients offshore for some outstanding crabbing success. Cheesman's 31-foot Boston Whaler is suited for offshore crabbing, and can handle seas most recreational crabbers wouldn't dream of tackling.

In addition to crabbing, Cheesman normally combines the outing with bottom fishing. Tossing the pots overboard, bottom fishing is often only minutes away in most areas, making routine checks of the crab pots easy.

Seasports I has also had many productive offshore trips at night, when perfectly calm seas and a full moon create optimal nocturnal crabbing conditions off the Oregon Coast. By affixing a glow stick to the surface buoy marker, locating your pot is easy. But Cheesman cautions people not to partake in such extreme crabbing if they're not thoroughly prepared and

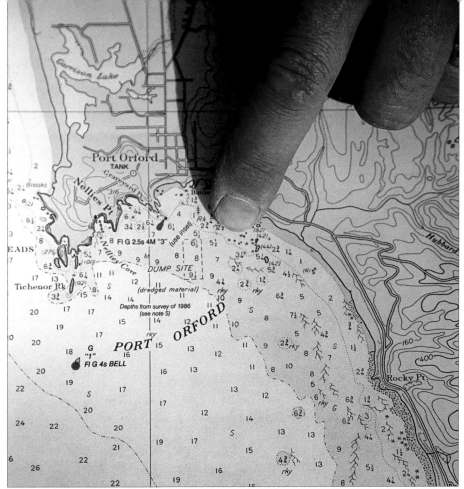

Working offshore is one of the best-kept secrets in the recreational crabbing world. You don't have to go out far, and if weather conditions are closely monitored, this is a safe means to harvest many crabs.

have plenty of sea navigation experience behind them. When night crabbing offshore, radar equipment is a must, and no matter where it's done, night crabbers must know the area well. If offshore night crabbing is new to you, hiring a guide the first time around is wise. Some Oregon bays are ideal for night crabbing, where city and residential lights help maintain bearings, and the waters are typically more calm. It should be noted that tending nighttime crab pots is prohibited in some states and select waters, so check local regulations.

If guided trips are not of interest, private vessels worthy of tackling offshore waters can find good success. Be certain your boat is properly equipped for offshore crabbing, and again, that operating skills and boat knowledge are honed. Know that ocean conditions can change in a moment's notice, and that circumstances in any given body of water may vary from day to day. Being aware and respectful of all viable ocean conditions will not only result in a safer, more enjoyable experience, it will produce quality crabs unlike anything you've seen inside bays.

CHAPTER 7

RAKING & DIP NETTING

One of my fondest childhood crabbing memories takes me back to one morning when a minus tide sucked the water from an Oregon bay. Admittedly, it happened by accident, as is so often the case among youngsters exploring their world, but when I unsuspectingly unearthed a hidden crab, the allure of the unknown further took hold within.

Dad was with me, raking cockles as I picked up seashells and fooled with other exposed sea life. Then, in a shallow pool, a faint, horizontal line in the sand caught my attention. Poking it with a stick, two round objects began moving about in robotic-like fashion. Enough pestering caused the stalked eyes to retract which, of course, engrossed me even more. Wedging my stick ever deeper, the two faint eyes and horizontal line popped to life as a big Dungeness shot from his protective lair. Not only was this crab a male, but a nice keeper at that. He was my first solo-catch and kept me wanting more.

Raking crabs is nothing new to sportsmen. During extreme minus tides, scores of people can be seen raking crabs in sandy depressions. When tides go out, crabs will hug the bottom, burying themselves in the sand to prevent being carried

Standard garden rakes are all that's needed for raking crabs, though the longer-tined version is preferred by some.

away. Locating these little holding spots can deliver a surprising number of crabs. In fact, on that morning when I discovered my first crab, Dad and I not only raked in our limits of clams, but took several nice Dungeness crabs as well.

Standard garden rakes work well, though longer-pronged versions prove more productive when probing for crabs. With a rake, bucket and hip boots, you're set. You may even choose to forego the boots, opting for a wet-wading adventure instead, something kids love.

The best time to rake for crabs is on the edge of outgoing tides, on through the slack low. The greater the minus tides the better, not only for exposing more crab holes, but in allotting more time to rake.

Finding buried crabs is wherein the challenge lies, and what makes this aspect of the sport so inviting. Blindly raking is a tactic adopted by many crabbers, taking caution not to damage the shells of crabs. When standing along the upper edge of a depression, insert the forks of the rake into the sand as far out as you can reach. Slowly pull the rake toward you, hoping to turn a crab by coming into contact with its legs or carapace.

Care must be taken to gently move the rake when blind-raking, so as not to damage the crab's shell. Remember, females and undersized crabs and soft-shell specimens are off limits, and wantonly damaging such creatures can result in a lofty fine.

But, if you know what you're looking for, raking can be done selectively. Rather than blindly raking through the sand, search for signs that crabs are present. Indications include exposed body parts and where the sand has sloughed off, over the front of a buried crab. Crabs bury themselves into these holes by backing their way into the sand. Their body position is typically horizontal to the sea floor, or at a slight angle respective to the sand

Raking in minus tides is a fun and productive means by which to collect crabs.

in which they seek refuge. Oftentimes, exposed eyes are what initially capture the attention of intent crab rakers. But look for more than body parts.

As a crab backs into the sand, the grains above the crab often fall, or slough off the front of its carapace. This often results in a horizontal line of sand which builds up in front of the crab. Depending on the type of sand, a color variation may also exist between that sand which has sloughed off a crab, or that covers its back, and the sand surrounding it. For instance, I've found crabs because the sand over their backs was distinctly lighter in color than the surrounding sand. Once you locate a crab in this way, finding successive crabs becomes easier.

Having visually located a buried crab, simply slip the rake beneath it and gently lift. This method of seeking out and selectively raking crabs results in no physical harm to the crab, and is actually a fun challenge of the sport to try and master.

If in areas where eelgrass prevails, wading through lagoons at low tide and dip-netting crabs can be very successful. Crabs thrive in eelgrass, where they often retreat during low tides. Crabbers employing the use of a dip net, scooping through the grass as they go, can be rewarded with generous catches. Towing a gunny sack in which to store your catch allows freedom of both hands to scoop. Dip netting is popular in selective bays harboring an eelgrass habitat; Dungeness and Birch Bay are among the most productive in Washington. I've found prime dip netting in parts of Alaska and coastal inlets around British Columbia's Inside Passage as well.

Raking and dip-netting Dungeness crabs is stress-free and fosters a level of involvement among children like no other form of recreational crabbing can. A major precautionary requirement is to keep an eye on incoming tides, so as not to be cut off from land. It's also important to know what the substrate is like in the area you plan on working.

Inquiring at local marinas as to the raking and dip-netting conditions to be expected is a good idea. Better yet, observe the local crowds. If plenty of people are working an area, chances are you're in the right spot. If the area looks crabby, but no one is within sight, it's for a reason. This is a sign to check with shop owners as to the safety measures to be taken and where to go for the best success.

If serious about raking or dip-netting crabs, hitting a low tide is the key in most areas.

RECREATIONAL DUNGENESS CRABBING

CHAPTER 8

ROD & REEL CRABBING

While utilizing a rod and reel to actively fish for crabs is not the most efficient means by which to harvest them, it can be intriguing entertainment for youngsters. When crabbing off docks, piers, and even in boats, there are times when the action slows. In order to prevent boredom overcoming children, give them a rod and reel and let 'em have at it.

While crabs are known to bite a baited fisherman's hook, this method should be avoided when targeting crabs for fear of permanently injuring the mouth parts of female and undersized male crabs. There are two basic contraptions allowing for the casting and catching of crabs on a sportfishing rod.

Crab snares, complete with a bait box, are not only captivating to curious young minds, they actually work. I once saw two huge, eight-inch crabs caught by two little girls off a dock with this device. Tying the bait box to a heavy monofilament or braided line, stuff it full of small, odd-sized bait and you're set. These crab snares can be purchased for under $10 in most marinas and sporting

The use of a rod, reel and a snare system can be effective,
and is something kids enjoy tinkering with.

Using a ball of old monofilament line with a bait and sinker attached to the center is another way to fish for crabs with rod and reel. As crabs seek the bait, their legs become entangled in the line.

as it seeks out the bait. Attaching a two-ounce sinker to the center of this "bird's nest," along with a morsel of bait, means you're ready for action.

Whichever setup you prefer, simply cast it out and wait. In calm settings, such as around moorages, you may be able to keep a tight line and actually detect a feeding crab on the other end. But more than likely, you'll need to quickly jerk the line up every few minutes to check for any action.

Because casting these contraptions may find you in rocks, using a heavy mainline—in the 20-pound class or greater—is recommended. Strong braided line is also a good choice for a mainline.

One area adults may want to consider casting for crabs is off jettys, whose rocky substrates make conventional crabbing with pots and rings very difficult. The key here is being able to cast beyond the rocks, followed by a swift retrieval, to prevent hangups in the rocks.

Casting for crabs is enjoyable for kids, piquing their curiosity as to what victims will fall for their bait. It's a great way for children to pass time when crabbing as a family from the docks, or when awaiting to pull pots in a boat.

However, don't be mislead into thinking crabbing with a rod and reel can be highly productive. While it does entertain young minds, it's not the method of choice to employ if catching scads of crabs is atop your agenda.

goods stores carrying standard crabbing equipment.

The other option involves more of a homemade snare system and requires only monofilament line and a sinker. The next time you change the line on a fishing rod, keep the tightly coiled, old line. Taking portions of the tangled line, tie it to the mainline of a fishing rod to be used for crab fishing. The idea is to create as many loops and snarls as possible, in which a crab will become tangled

CHAPTER 9

Diving For Crabs

If seeking the ultimate in extreme crabbing, head under water and go one-on-one with Mr. Dungeness. Capturing crabs with your hands is only one of the challenges facing divers, as first you must find them.

If you're truly set on learning about crabs, there's no better way than observing them in their natural environment—something only a fraction of crabbers have ever done. Freediving, or snorkeling, is one option, requiring nothing more than a snorkel, gloves, fins, weight belt and wetsuit. Freediving can be done near piers, docks, along the edges of rocky structures, and in shallow portions of any bay.

Visibility and tidal fluctuations are two factors freedivers must constantly monitor. The greater the visibility, the better the chances of finding crabs. If working bays with staunch tides, be cognizant of your surroundings at all times. Breath-hold diving in five to 50 feet of water can be productive, with 20 feet of depth being an optimal range.

Freediving can also be practiced offshore, when conditions are ideal. But if diving is what you desire, be it in bays or offshore, you won't be disappointed with the time and effort it takes to become certified.

Scuba diving for crabs not only puts you in their home, it opens up a whole new fascinating world few people know exists in Pacific waters. In addition to crabs, bottom fish, seals, whales and even sharks can be seen up close and personal.

Freediving, or snorkeling, for crabs is productive along jetties and places of structure.

Since establishing his Seasports Diving and Fishing Shop in 1982, Springfield, Oregon Captain John Cheesman has been certifying and taking divers to the sea. Cheesman and his instructional staff of professionals teach several classes each year, certifying divers on a regular basis. Many divers who've become certified through Seasports are hooked for life on this fascinating sport. A devotion to the sport of diving, combined with a zest to explore the unknown, will take divers into an alluring undersea fantasy world.

In addition to organizing routine dive trips off the Oregon and Washington coast, Cheesman regularly takes dedicated divers to such exotic locales as Fiji and Mexico. With dive shops situated throughout the Pacific Northwest, if you're serious about taking up this enthralling sport, now is the time.

"Diving for crabs adds a sense of awesome adventure that's addicting," offers Cheesman. "There's nothing like getting down, face to face with crabs and other ocean creatures, observing them in their natural environment. Catching crabs by hand may not be as easy as one thinks, especially with crabs so active on the bottom."

When diving for crabs, where you find them is a split—50% being buried, 50% scurrying about the ocean floor. As with other forms of recreational crabbing, diving for crabs is most productive during high slack because this is when crabs are more likely to be on the move and when they are most challenging to snatch. Once they detect an intruder, crabs can move surprisingly fast in their nimble, sideways, crab-like style. Once on the move, catching up with a scurrying crab will test even the most seasoned diver.

If crabs aren't out searching for food, they're tucked away in their sandy domain or snug against rocks. This is where a sharp eye and persistence will reward the diver. As discussed in Chapter 7, divers look for the same clues to a crab's presence as do people raking crabs. Protruding eyes, the edge of an exposed carapace and that faint line where sand has sloughed off a buried crab are all signs divers should key in on when looking for burrowed crabs.

When diving near rocky structures, concentrate on the vicinity where sand meets rock. Crabs will often back into the rocks of these zones, rather than burying themselves in the sand. Concentrating dives along structures such as jettys can be highly productive. Regardless of where you dive, clipping on a measuring device for immediate legal assessment of the crabs you grab, and a game bag to carry your catch, are two must-haves.

Offshore diving for crabs is fruitful in 10 to 70 feet of water, whenever there's good visibility. If there's 10 feet of visibility, diving for crabs can pay off, but when you get visibility conditions ranging from 15 feet upwards of

Bill Ebert dove deep for this pair of crabs.

RECREATIONAL DUNGENESS CRABBING

Diving is one of the most challenging approaches to gathering crabs, and takes you into a world of intrigue and mystery.

40 feet, the crabbing can be outstanding. Cheesman notes that he's hit many days with 100 feet of visibility off the Oregon Coast, thanks to good timing. He also points out that as long as the surge isn't bad, diving with a mere five feet of visibility can produce crabs.

Cheesman advises offshore divers to be on the lookout for longshore currents when crabbing. Though tidal flows offshore are not a factor, the presence of longshore currents means drift-diving is the only way to go. This activity requires the captain on board the vessel to monitor and flow with the divers below. As the current carries the divers, the captain pays attention to their bubbles, keeping with them at all times. Such currents will likely put the crabs down, requiring careful searching for buried quarry.

"Crabbing in longshore currents produces crabs, but I'll avoid diving when swells are high," suggests Cheesman. "The surge of big swells can stir up the bottom, forcing crabs to bury themselves in sand so as not to be carried away. You know when you're underwater, feeling the surge of swells, the crabs are also feeling it. During such swells, I'll head to the boat and spend time diving in the bays."

Being an experienced diver—knowing your gear and the area in which you'll be diving—is the first key to successful crabbing. Once you become certified, you must be dedicated and stay on top of things. The investment of time will be highly rewarded, for not only will your crabbing skills gain an edge, but the new underwater world that will open up to you will be spellbinding. One of nature's greatest wonders lies beneath the sea, and diving is the only way to fully experience it.

CHAPTER 10

CRABBING IN OREGON

Crabbing throughout the Beaver State is productive, though certain times of the year and specific locations may be better than others. No matter where in Oregon—or along the Pacific Coast—you crab, success may be dependent on several factors.

Ocean conditions, winter snowpack, spring runoff and seasonal rainfall can all impact crabbing success, as can salinity levels within any bay at any given time. In fact, some of these natural elements impact even neighboring estuaries differently, rendering some bays better for crabbing than others.

While several bays exist along the Oregon Coast, we won't go into detail on every one. Instead, we'll take a look at the more prominent crabbing estuaries and what can be expected of them. This does not mean bays and ports lacking mention are not worth visiting, as they too are regarded as viable crab fisheries in their own right.

If searching for Oregon's premier crabbing locale, two bays come to mind. Coos Bay, out of Charleston, is second only in size to the Columbia. This estuary is among my favorite, for I've never left its waters without a bountiful catch of crabs. Crabbing from the mouth of the bay all the way up to Empire is productive, with an abundance of scrumptious red rock crabs also readily available.

Winchester Bay, however, is my top where-to place when it comes to crabbing. Perhaps it's because there are so many other things to do at this unique

Oregon's many protected bays offer excellent crabbing.

bay, be it fishing, clamming or sight-seeing. The mouth of the mighty Umpqua River enters the ocean here, and is teaming with abundant life. Dropping the pots while fishing for fall chinook, silvers, and perch is the norm, as crabbing can be good here through the entire spring, well into winter. In 2002, a crab sporting a $10,000 price tag was placed in these waters, part of the annual Crab Bounty Hunt that runs through August and September. In addition to the big-money crab, other crabs are tagged with prizes, just waiting to be caught.

Siuslaw Bay, out of Florence, is also a good crabbing estuary. The consistency of the crabbing to be had here is its stronghold, where success is fairly regular from April through October. Crabbing is good from the Coast Guard station, on out to the jetties.

Alsea Bay, out of Waldport, is a good little crabbing estuary, offering rakers, dock crabbers, and boaters high odds of finding what they're looking for. Continuing up the coast, Newport's Yaquina Bay is atop many peoples' lists as the prime crabbing bay in Oregon. Crabbing here is good year-round, with the deeper channels in the lower section of the bay being most congenial.

Tillamook Bay has to be classified among Oregon's great crabbing bays, and success can be had here throughout the year. Due to the amount of water dumping into the bay—where five rivers come together—crabs can head to the sea during times of heavy rains. To the north of Tillamook, Nehalem Bay also produces crabs the entire year, with late summer and fall being most lucrative.

Oregon now requires the purchase of a shellfish license for recreational crabbing. With a 5 3/4 inches size limit on male Dungeness crabs, 12 being the daily catch limit, there are no size or sex restrictions

placed on red rock crabs, only that 24 is the limit. Crabs may be taken with the use of pots, rings or baited lines, but only three of these in any combination at any one time may be used by a single person. As rules and regulations are forever changing, sportsmen are advised to refer to the latest edition of the Oregon Sport Fishing Regulations before heading afield.

To learn more about crabbing in Oregon, in either of the locations touched upon here, or those that have not received mention, call the state's general information line and request the number for the Chamber of Commerce in the town or city nearest where you wish to crab. They can provide you with listings for local marinas, moorage facilities, campgrounds and RV parks. State Fish and Wildlife officials are another valuable resource for learning about crabbing along the Oregon Coast.

CHAPTER 11

CRABBING IN WASHINGTON

Trying to document all of the good crabbing locations in the state of Washington is a task nearly requiring a book in itself. To try and do so here would be an injustice to all that's available in this great state, for, inevitably, some prime sites would be neglected.

Nevertheless, there are some marine areas and special sites requiring mention, but do not limit your crab quest to these locales. There are numerous bays and tidal zones worthy of crabbing, be it by diving, tossing rings from a boat or dock, or by dip netting.

The beauty of Washington's shellfish resources is that they are closely managed thanks to funding earmarked for such care. Through the mandatory purchase of a shellfish license, valuable dollars annually go to the proper management and preservation of

Washington's shellfish. Many Oregon sportsmen and fish and wildlife authorities hope their state will follow suit, and one glance at Washington's Sport Fishing Regulations and website devoted to this fishery will tell you why.

These comprehensive guides feature technical information so complete, there's no reason for any crabbing fan to be in violation of any state law. Likewise, one must take the time to thoroughly read and understand the laws as they appear in the regulations booklet. There is also a toll-free information hotline (866-880-5431) to call for further clarification and up-to-date regulation adjustments.

Three points of interest exist which Washington crabbers will want to know about. A shellfish license is required for crabbers in this state, and it must be displayed on

Proper management means there are some magnum-size Dungeness crabs to be had in Washington waters.

your person while crabbing or transporting caught crabs. In addition to a shellfish license, a Catch Record Card is required, on which all caught Dungeness crabs are to be recorded. Finally, when crabbing from a boat, a specialized crab pot buoy is required. This half red, half white buoy must show both colors when floating, and needs to have scribed on it in permanent ink, one person's name and complete address. Below the buoy, lines must be sufficiently weighted to prevent floating to the surface and getting caught in boat propellers.

At the time of this writing, two units of gear (a unit consisting of one star trap, one pot or one ring net) per person are allowed for the taking of crabs in all coastal waters, Puget Sound and Hood Canal. Three total units of gear per person can be used in the mouth of the Columbia, upstream of the Buoy 10 line.

There are other, area-specific regulations crabbers need to be aware of. For instance, while night crabbing is legal in Oregon, crab pots may not be tended from a vessel at night in the state of Washington. To learn more about these and other statewide gear rules, consult the most recent issue of the Washington Sport Fishing Rules.

Puget Sound hosts a plethora of crabbing opportunities, as the many islands and protected bays create ideal Dungeness crab habitat. On the northern end of Camano Island, Utsalady Bay is a good location to hit. On the southern reaches of Whidbey Island, Possession Point, Useless Bay and Holmes Harbor all contain good crabbing. Across from these sites, near Everett, East Port Susan and Port Garner are proven crab producers.

Working up the sound, Padilla and Fidalgo bays, near Anacortes are good bets, as is Samish Bay. Birch Bay, off Neptune Beach and just north of Lummi Island, is also a popular crabbing site. Several year-round crabbing opportunities exist in the San Juan, Lopez, Shaw and Orcas islands region, and should not go overlooked.

On the sound side of the Olympic Peninsula, Hood Canal is one of Washington's most famous crabbing destinations. Dungeness Bay is also popular, and marks the site from whence these famous crabs derived their name.

Grays Harbor and Willapa Bay, along the southwestern shores of the state, also host solid crabbing opportunities. Wildlife agencies near these destinations can direct sportsmen to more specific, crab-producing sites.

Dip netting is a popular method of take in Washington, and crabbers wishing to try their luck at this sport should turn to Port Gardner, off the Everett Jetty. Other hotspots include Lummi and Padilla bays, Whidbey and Camano islands and Port Susan. Dungeness Bay and Birch Bay are also well known for their short-handled dip-netting opportunities.

For more information on Washington crabbing opportunities, refer to the appendix.

CHAPTER 12

CLEANING & PREPARING YOUR CATCH

Once you've attained a limit of crabs, the work begins. Cleaning and preparing crabs can be as enjoyable of an experience as you choose to make it. But prior to cleaning crabs, it's imperative to consider the presence of harmful bacteria and biotoxins in their bodies, for being aware of such effects may determine how you choose to prepare your catch.

Due to increased levels of pollution and industrial byproducts making their way into our oceans, shellfish can become exposed to and contaminated with unnatural chemicals, bacteria, biotoxins and even viruses. The consumption of contaminated shellfish can

While crabbing, occasionally splash your catch with water or cover with a wet towel. Placing them in water will suffocate them, as they use up the oxygen too rapidly.

A pot full of crabs like this is what every serious crabber yearns for.

lead to serious illness, even death. Paralytic Shellfish Poisoning (PSP), dubbed "red tide" is transmitted to shellfish as they consume algae containing potentially lethal biotoxins. If, after eating shellfish, you experience numbing lips, tongue and a tingling sensation in the extremities, followed by possible loss of muscle control and breathing difficulty, seek immediate medical assistance. Amnesic Shellfish Poisoning (ASP) is another potentially harmful biotoxin consumed by shellfish that can pass to humans. Abdominal cramps, diarrhea, vomiting, dizziness and loss of memory are symptoms of this disease.

But don't let these disorders keep you from crabbing. Regions in which shellfish are known to carry these

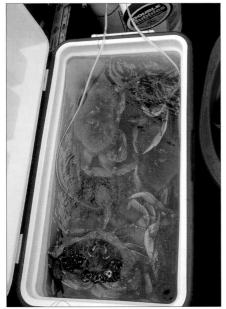

Aerators are ideal for keeping crabs alive all day long. Given the increased appearance of biotoxins, more and more crabbers are going this route to ensure their catch stays lively.

after being caught, the likelihood of exposure to any such disease is unlikely.

It should be noted that rinsing and freezing crabs does not destroy the biotoxins within. Nor does cooking crabs rid them of biotoxins, but it does help prevent illnesses caused by naturally occurring bacteria or bacteria that has developed due to pollution. For these reasons, it's imperative to clean crabs prior to cooking them, and to thoroughly cook them prior to consumption. Only the meat should be consumed in crabs, not their internal organs.

I recall when I was a kid, our neighbor would bring home a load of crabs, crack the carapace off the cooked ones and spoon out the hepatopancreas, or "crab butter," and consume every drop. The buttery flavor of this fat is appealing to the pallet, but should not be eaten, no matter how inviting.

The care of crabs begins the moment you catch them. Avoid putting them in water, as they will consume the oxygen and drown. Instead, place the crabs in a

diseases are promptly closed by state authorities. And, if handled properly

Crab-cooking facilities are available near most good crabbing waters.

bucket or cooler, periodically splashing salt water over them or keeping a moistened towel or gunny sack draped over top. By keeping them moist and out of direct sunlight, they will live for several hours, even out of the water.

The use of aerators to keep crabs alive is growing in popularity. If you wish to make certain your crabs stay fresh and alive during a day on the water, an aerator is the way to go. Placed in a large cooler, simply change out the water a couple times a day to keep it fresh. At the end of the day the crabs will be as lively as when they were pulled from the ocean, leaving no question as to their health status.

That said, there are two ways to go about processing your catch: doing it yourself or paying someone a nominal fee to take care of it. In most ports where crabbing exists, shops with commercial cookers are often readily accessible. Giving these folks your catch and having them cleaned and cooked is the

way to go. For around $5.00, a limit of crabs can be cleaned, cooked and placed on ice. I like having crabs cooked while I'm cleaning the boat and all the gear. These marinas are set up to quickly and efficiently process your crabs, saving you valued time and effort.

However, there are times when you pull into port and find these shops closed. You may also opt for cooking the crabs yourself, something that's a blast with a large group of people gathered around a fire on the beach.

Two popular methods of cleaning crabs include cooking them whole, then cleaning them, or cleaning them first, then cooking them. I prefer the latter because of the health concerns mentioned above.

If, however, you prefer to cook crabs whole, make absolutely certain every crab tossed into the pot is done so alive. If even one crab is dead, the bacteria and toxins released from it can cause serious illness. Some people argue that the best

If boiling crabs whole, make certain they are alive before tossing them in. If they are dead, dangerous biotoxins may leach into the meat, causing serious illness.

way to cook a crab to capture its full flavor, is to do so whole, claiming the crab butter cooks its way into the meat. With the biotoxins housed in these organs, that's precisely what you don't want. I've had crabs cooked whole and in parts, and can decipher no difference in taste quality. If it's the butter flavor you desire, consider adding creamy butter when you sit down at the table.

If you have a long drive home and won't get to the cooking until the following day, it's imperative to take measures to keep the crabs alive if cooking them whole. A good way is to wrap them in wet towels or newspapers and place them in the refrigerator or atop ice in a cooler. If placing in the cooler, make sure the ice has a thick layer of newspapers between it and the crabs. You don't want this ice melting and the crabs swimming in the water. If you have several crabs, they can be kept in a

After cooking, immediately douse crabs in cold water and place on ice to stop the cooking process.

large-capacity cooler with an aerator that will keep them alive.

Before cooking crabs whole, make sure they are alive by poking an eye or an antenna. These sensitive organs should move when stimulated. If they appear sluggish, crabs can be renewed by quickly submerging them in cold water. Once the whole crab has been cooked, pry off the carapace, break the crab in half and thoroughly clean it. Make sure to remove the gills and visceral mass, where harmful toxins are harbored.

If cooking your crabs whole, bring the salt water to a boil, then place the crabs in the pot. Bring the contents to a boil once again, allowing the crabs to cook for 20 minutes. Take the crabs from the pot, let cool and remove the shells and all internal contents. If you

When cooking crabs, bring the water to a boil, add the crabs, then once again bring to a boil.

have more crabs to cook, repeat the process with a fresh supply of salt water—avoid using the smelly water to cook a second batch of crabs. When the crabs are done cooking, cover them in cold water or ice. Not only does cold water stop the cooking process, it swiftly cools the meat, causing the muscles to retract away from the shell, making for easier cleaning.

In my opinion, cleaning a crab prior to cooking it is the only way to go. This leaves no room for doubt as to its edibility. Begin with a live crab, turning it on its back. Take a good-size knife, such as a fillet knife, and place the blade in the center of the crab, firmly against the abdomen. With a hammer or mallet, drive the blade through the shell, breaking the abdomen. This blow not only kills the crab, it makes for easier separation of the meat from the carapace. Pull the two halves of the body—complete with attached legs—away from the carapace.

You're now left holding two halves of the crab: legs, pincers and all. Remove the gills by hand, and vigorously

1. Using a knife and mallet is an efficient way to kill and clean a crab prior to cooking.

2. Removing the halves of the crab from the carapace, legs and all, is the next step in the cleaning stage.

3. Remove the gills and remaining internal organs before cooking.

4. Shake or rinse free any visceral mass, then it's ready for the cooker.

RECREATIONAL DUNGENESS CRABBING

shake the remaining visceral mass free. A quick flick of the wrist will shake the internal mass free. Give the halves a quick rinse in water and they are ready to be cooked.

If at the beach, pure salt water from the open ocean is the best medium in which to cook crabs, as it contains optimal salt content. If cooking at home, mixing one cup rock salt to one gallon of fresh water closely matches the salinity level of sea water. While cleaning the crabs, start the water boiling. Once the water starts to boil, add the crabs.

With the crabs in the pot, allow the water to once again reach the boiling point and cook for 11 minutes. At the end of 11 minutes of boiling, the crab halves are finished cooking. Remove the cooked crabs, place them in a cold water bath, then place on ice. Cooking crabs in this way is clean, produces considerably less odor, and allows you to accommodate more crabs compared to cooking them whole.

Freezing crab meat in saltwater is a two-step process, but preserves the taste of the meat surprisingly well.

Crabs are delectable when the meat is warm, fresh from the cooker. But if you're transporting cooked crab, or holding it over for a day, keep it chilled, as crab meat perishes rapidly. Placing crabs on ice or in the refrigerator is ideal for preserving the meat, where it can be eaten fresh within the first 24 hours. Beyond one day, it's advisable to freeze the meat. If you have more meat than can be consumed, a good way to freeze it is in a saltwater solution.

With the one-cup-rock-salt-to-one gallon-of-freshwater ratio, an ideal freezing bath can be attained. Loosely place the crab into small, plastic containers, filling to within an inch of the top with salt water. The meat will float in this solution, so don't pack it down. Once frozen, top-off the container with the salt water, covering the exposed meat. Crab meat will keep this way for up to six months and yield very tasty meat, though the sooner you can eat it, the better its overall quality.

Cleaned crabs are boiled for 11 minutes, emerging ready to eat.

CHAPTER 13

FAVORITE CRAB RECIPES

While the preferred way to eat crab is fresh from the shell, there's only so much of this a person's stomach can comfortably accommodate. Spreading out a thick layer of newspapers atop the kitchen table, getting elbow-deep in shucking crabs is the whole impetus behind crabbing in the first place. Dipping freshly-shelled crabs into homemade sauces or melted garlic butter is beyond delectable.

But if you find yourself with a crabmeat surplus, there are ways of preparing it that will keep you wanting more.

Because I have the luxury of being married to an award-winning cook, I've been exposed to eating crab beyond the simple cook-and-shuck phase. While there are many fine recipes out there, the following are favorites of our family, and ones I'm sure you'll enjoy.

There's nothing better than getting elbow-deep in fresh, shucked crab.

Crab Salad

Crab salads offer a tasty alternative.

Crab Lasagna

The author's favorite recipe, crab lasagna, is something every crab-lover must try.

- 1/2 cup butter
- 3 cloves chopped garlic
- 1/2 cup flour
- 2 cups milk
- 1 14 oz. can chicken broth
- 2 cups cottage cheese
- 1 egg
- 2 tablespoons fresh chopped parsley
- 1/2 teaspoon lemon pepper
- 9 uncooked lasagna noodles
- 2 cups grated mozzarella cheese
- 1/2 cup parmesan cheese
- 3 cups fresh or thawed, shelled crab meat

Melt butter in a medium-size saucepan on medium-low heat. Lightly sauté garlic and add flour, stirring constantly with a wire whisk. When mixture begins to bubble, turn heat to low and slowly add the milk and chicken broth. Return the mixture to a boil until thick, 1-2 minutes, stirring constantly. Remove from heat and set aside. In a separate bowl mix the cottage cheese, egg, parsley and lemon pepper. In a 9" x 13" casserole dish, spread enough of the white sauce to coat the bottom of the pan. Layer with 3 uncooked lasagna noodles, 1/3 of the cottage cheese mixture, 1/3 of the crab, 1/3 of the mozzarella and parmesan cheeses. Repeat the layering 2 more times, making sure cheese is the final layer. Bake, uncovered at 350º for 50-60 minutes. Let stand at least 10 minutes before serving. This recipe can be prepared ahead and refrigerated uncooked for up to 12 hours. Let sit at room temperature for 20 minutes before baking.

Crab Quiche

Crab quiche is easy, nutritious and makes a great meal for crab lovers.

- 1 10-inch uncooked pie crust
- 6 eggs
- 2/3 cup milk
- 1/2 teaspoon onion salt
- 1/4 teaspoon black pepper

- 2 cups fresh or thawed, shelled crab meat
- 1/2 cup grated cheddar cheese
- 1/2 cup grated jack cheese
- 1 tablespoon fresh, chopped basil

Beat eggs, milk, salt and pepper together, set aside. Place the uncooked pie crust into a pie pan. Sprinkle crab meat and basil evenly in the pie shell. Sprinkle cheddar and jack cheeses over the crab meat. Pour egg mixture over everything in the pie pan. Bake at 350° for 35-45 minutes or until set and golden brown.

Crab-Stuffed Mushrooms

Stuffed mushrooms are a tasty appetizer everyone is sure to enjoy.

- 30-35 medium mushrooms
- 1/2 cup butter
- 1/4 cup finely chopped onion
- 2 cloves minced garlic

- 3/4 cup bread crumbs
- 1/2 teaspoon Italian seasoning
- 1 cup finely chopped fresh or thawed, crab meat
- 1/2 cup parmesan cheese

Clean mushrooms and remove stems. Place mushrooms on a greased cookie sheet and set aside. Melt butter in a medium-size saucepan on medium-low heat. Sauté onions until translucent, add garlic and lightly sauté. Remove from heat and add bread crumbs, Italian seasoning, crab meat and parmesan cheese, mixing well. Generously fill mushroom caps with the mixture, packing it down. Broil on low for 5-7 minutes, watching closely. Garnish with finely chopped tomatoes and fresh basil. Crab filling can be refrigerated for up to two days prior to cooking.

RECREATIONAL DUNGENESS CRABBING

Crab Fritters

Crab fritters nicely accent the natural taste of the meat.

- 2 cups white flour
- 2 teaspoons baking powder
- 2 teaspoons salt
- 4 eggs
- 1 cup milk
- 2 teaspoons vegetable oil
- 4 cups fresh or thawed shelled crab meat
- vegetable oil for frying

Mix the dry ingredients in a medium-size mixing bowl. Make a well in the center and add eggs, milk and vegetable oil. Mix thoroughly with a spoon until smooth, do not overbeat. Gently fold shelled crab meat into the batter mixture. Using an electric frying pan, add 1 1/2 inches of oil to the pan. Heat the oil to 350°. Using a large tablespoon, drop the fritters carefully into the oil and fry until golden brown on each side, turning once (approximately 2 minutes on each side). Drain on a wire rack or paper towels. Serve hot with dip (mix of 3 parts mayonnaise to 1 part ketchup).

Crab Puffs

Crab puffs are a great way to prepare the scrumptious meat.

- 1 cup 7-Up
- 1/2 cup butter or margarine
- 1 cup flour
- 4 large eggs
- 1 1/2 cups fresh or thawed, shelled crab meat

- 1 8-ounce package whipped cream cheese (at room temperature)
- 1/4 teaspoon salt
- 1/4 teaspoon pepper
- 2 tablespoons finely sliced green onion

Bring 7-Up and butter to a boil in a medium saucepan. Add flour. Remove from heat. Add eggs one at a time and beat after each. Drop the mixture, by teaspoonful, on a cookie sheet. Bake at 350° for about 10 minutes (watch closely). They should be lightly browned on the top. Let the puffs cool. Mix crab, cream cheese, salt, pepper and green onion together. Slice puffs in half and stuff with crab filling. Makes 25-30 puffs. Serve immediately or keep refrigerated.

Nutritional Information

Dungeness crab is an excellent source of quality protein. While maintaining a low fat and caloric content, it contains all of the essential amino acids. Valued minerals such as calcium, copper, iron, magnesium and zinc are found in crab, making it a favorite among health-conscious consumers.

Following is a breakdown of the nutritional value of Dungeness crab. This is based on a cooked, edible portion of meat with a serving size of three ounces. The information is provided by the Food Processor computerized nutrition system, ESHA Research in Salem, Oregon.

Calories	93.6
Protein	19 g.
Total Fat	1.06 g.
Saturated	0.143 g.
Monounsaturated	0.182 g.
Polyunsaturated	0.346 g.
Carbohydrates	0.808 g.
Cholesterol	64.6 mg.
Magnesium	49.3 mg.
Potassium	347 mg.
Sodium	321 mg.

CONCLUSION

Three generations of the author's family enjoy a day of crabbing, something they always look forward to.

Some 17,000 tons of Dungeness crab valued at tens of millions of dollars are annually harvested by commercial crabbers from California to Alaska. These numbers alone speak for the demand placed on crabs by seafood lovers. But catching them for yourself is much more rewarding than buying them at the local market.

The joys to be had through recreational crabbing are unlike any other in the outdoors. While I truly enjoy traveling the world on big-game hunts and exotic fishing trips, I always look forward with eager anticipation to the times I get to spend crabbing along the Pacific Coast. Be it in Alaska or my home state of Oregon, pursuing Dungeness crabs is a thrill, and provides a sense of adventure that is unattainable through hunting on land and fishing in rivers.

Not only are crabs a delicacy sportsmen have the wonderful opportunity to partake in harvesting, but they lure you into a world you might not otherwise venture. Those of us fortunate enough to live near where

The author (left) and Jason Reed enjoy a calm day on the water. Getting together with friends is one of the joys of recreational crabbing.

crabbing is readily attainable must be thankful for the blessing at our fingertips.

But more than the palatable fantasies these shelled creatures fulfill, it's their degree of susceptibility sportsmen find appealing. Catching crabs is not rocket science. With some general knowledge of crabs and their behavior, along with a working sense of the equipment related to the sport, anyone with the desire can expect success. Herein lies the objective of this book.

Of course, crabbing success can be dependent upon a heightened level of respect for the sea and its natural resources. By abiding by all laws, being aware of what the sea is capable of, and respecting fellow sportsmen,

Matt and Stacy Haugen have been crabbing the Oregon coast for years. Now their children, Drew and Anna, enjoy the family outings.

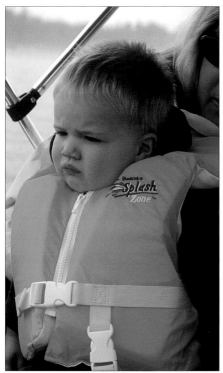

The author and his wife introduced their son Braxton to crabbing at 17 months of age. It's never too early to start.

the future of this unique fishery will be preserved and passed on to future generations.

It is my fondest hope that the information found within these pages will entice people to get out and experience, firsthand, what crabbing is all about. If new to the sport, I hope this book will set you on your way to a newfound, lifelong pastime.

As a new generation of young sportsmen make their way into the Haugen family, I'm counting the days when my sons will experience the joy of hoisting their first pot full of crabs to the surface. While there's nothing like crabbing, there's truly nothing that compares to crabbing as a family; only then can the total impact of this fine sport be realized.

APPENDIX

Catcher Company (Smelly Jelly)
5285 N.E. Elam Young Parkway
Suite B700
Hillsboro, OR 97124
(503) 648-2643

Bob Cobb's Reel Fishing
Reedsport, Oregon
877-271-3850
reelfishing@harborside.com

John Cheesman
Seasports, Inc. Diving & Fishing
1147 Main Street
Springfield, OR 97477
541-726-2055
john@seasportsoregon.com
www.seasportsoregon.com

Oregon Department of Fish & Wildlife
Main Office
   2501 SW First Avenue
   P.O. Box 59
   Portland, OR 97207-0059
   (503) 872-5268
   www.dfw.state.or.us

Regional Office
   2040 SE Marine Science Drive
   Newport, OR 97365
   (541) 867-4741

Oregon Shellfish Health Advisories
(503) 986-4728

Patrick Roelle
Fishpatrick's Guide Service
(541)744-8093
www.fishpatrick.com

Patrick Sullivan
Sully's Guide Service
86054 Dery Road
Pleasant Hill, OR 97455
(541)747-8874
pat@gosullys.com
www.gosullys.com

Washington Department of Fish & Wildlife
Main Office
   600 Capitol Way N
   Olympia, WA 98501-1091
   (360) 902-2700
   www.wa.gov/wdfw/

Field Office
   Willapa Bay
   267th and Sandridge Road
   Nahcotta, WA 98637
   (360) 665-4166

Washington State Shellfish Rule Change Hotline
1-866-880-5431

Washington State Marine Toxins Hotline
1-800-562-5632
www.doh.wa.gov/ehp/sf/biotoxin.htm